How to Make Driver's Licenses and Other ID on Your Home Computer

How to Make Driver's Licenses and Other ID on Your Home Computer

by Max Forgé

Loompanics Unlimited
Port Townsend, Washington

This book is sold for informational purposes only. Neither the author nor the publisher will be held accountable for the use or misuse of the information contained in this book.

How to Make Driver's Licenses and Other ID on Your Home Computer
© 1999 by Max Forgé

All rights reserved. No part of this book may be reproduced or stored in any form whatsoever without the prior written consent of the publisher. Reviews may quote brief passages without the written consent of the publisher as long as proper credit is given.

Published by:
Loompanics Unlimited
PO Box 1197
Port Townsend, WA 98368

Loompanics Unlimited is a division of Loompanics Enterprises, Inc.
(360) 385-2230
E-mail: loompanx@olympus.net
Web site: www.loompanics.com

Illustrations by Jim B.

ISBN 1-55950-194-4
Library of Congress Card Catalog 99-63626

Contents

Introduction 1
Definitions 3
Chapter One
   Required Equipment and Suppliers 5
Chapter Two
   Configuring Photoshop 11
Chapter Three
   Acquiring the License Template 19
Chapter Four
   Scanning the License and Preparing
   the License Template 23
Chapter Five
   Getting a License Template on the Internet 35
Chapter Six
   Adding the Picture 39
Chapter Seven
   License Font Identification 49
Chapter Eight
   License Personalization 53
Chapter Nine
   Holograms 59
Chapter Ten
   License Structure 61

Chapter Eleven
  Printing, Cutting, and Laminating
  Structure One Licenses 65

Chapter Twelve
  Printing, Cutting, and Laminating
  Structure Two Licenses 75

Chapter Thirteen
  Printing, Cutting, and Laminating
  Structure Three Licenses 83

Chapter Fourteen
  Back-up ID 91

Chapter Fifteen
  Evaluating the Completed License:
  Is It Good Enough? 95

Chapter Sixteen
  Using the License Intelligently 99

Appendix A 101

Introduction

The driver's license has become America's primary form of identification. These days it is impossible to cash a check, open a bank account, rent a mailbox or buy a beer without one. While some individuals find it annoying that they must show their license at every turn, I find it liberating! The common belief that a license is extremely difficult to duplicate has been very empowering to those of us who know better.

This book discusses the techniques developed during my four years of manufacturing fake ID with my home computer. It provides a detailed description of the equipment, software, and assembly of widely accepted fake ID. While this book focuses primarily on driver's licenses, its techniques can be easily applied to the manufacture of almost any form of identification or document.

Editor's Note: This book is in no way intended to be an endorsement for any printers or software mentioned. The author uses a specific program and mentions specific brands of printers, laminators, and supplies because they were, in his opinion, the best available for the purpose outlined.

Definitions

Throughout the book, the following terms will be used:

- **Physical license**: The actual license that is being counterfeited.
- **License template**: The computer copy of the physical license.
- **Information card**: The paper or Teslin with a picture and personal information printed on it.

Quick Reference

Appendix A contains annotated printouts of the Photoshop menus and tools used in this book.

Chapter One
Required Equipment and Suppliers

Chapter One
Required Equipment and Suppliers

This chapter details the equipment required to manufacture counterfeit licenses.

How to Make Driver's Licenses and Other ID
on Your Home Computer

The Printer

The printer is the most critical piece of license-counterfeiting equipment. If the printer isn't good, the license won't be either, regardless of how much money was invested in the other system components.

At a minimum, a 600 x 600 DPI, color ink-jet printer is required. Of course, all printers are not created equal. The following printers have distinguished themselves as being a cut above the rest.

RECOMMENDED EQUIPMENT		
Make/Model Number	Price	Comments
EPSON 600/800	$220/$250	720 x 1440 DPI. Good quality.
EPSON 740	$240	720 x 1440 DPI. Better color than the EPSON 600/800.
ALPS MD-1300	$350	1400 x 1400 DPI. Excellent quality. Prints metallic inks. Is capable of printing simulated holograms with metallic ink.
ALPS MD-5000	$500	2400 x 2400 DPI. Excellent quality. Prints metallic inks. Foil printing. Is capable of printing simulated holograms with metallic ink.

Chapter One
Required Equipment and Suppliers

The Scanner

The difference between a $70 bargain-basement scanner and a $400 scanner is very noticeable. Either one will ultimately work, but it will take a lot more failed attempts before an adequate scan is achieved on a cheap scanner.

At a minimum, a 300 x 600 DPI 30-bit scanner is required, but for just $50 more, a 600 x 1200 DPI 36-bit scanner is preferred. The following scanners are feature-packed and reasonably priced.

RECOMMENDED EQUIPMENT		
Make/Model Number	Price	Comments
UMAX ASTRA 1220P	$120	600 x 1200 DPI, 36-bit. Very good scan. Excellent color.
UMAX ASTRA 2400S	$400	1200 x 2400 DPI, 36-bit. Excellent scan and color.

The Laminator

Office supply stores, such as Staples and Office Depot, sell card-sized laminators for about $45. It would be very easy to spend more but don't bother, as the less expensive ones do a great job. The GBC DocuSeal 40 is excellent for this application.

How to Make Driver's Licenses and Other ID on Your Home Computer

---

LAMINATOR ALTERNATIVE?

There is no alternative to a laminator. Often, unknowledgeable people claim that self-sealing laminates eliminate the need for a laminator. Don't listen! Self-sealing laminates begin to delaminate almost immediately — one quick twist by a suspicious bouncer and the ID will disintegrate.

The Software

A copy of Adobe Photoshop 4.0 or 4.1 is required. Photoshop is one of the most heavily pirated pieces of software in history. It can be found at almost every WAREZ site on the Web or at the local software store for $550. Do not attempt to use any program other than Photoshop; it is the best for this kind of work. This book uses Photoshop exclusively.

FINDING WAREZ SITES CONTAINING PHOTOSHOP

1. Log onto the Internet.
2. Go to http://www.hotbot.com.
3. Search for "WAREZ and Photoshop."
4. Follow the links to the identified sites.
5. Download Photoshop (NOTE: Photoshop is VERY large — expect to spend several hours downloading this file.).

The Computer

The better the computer, the easier it will be to manipulate the scanned images. At a minimum, a PC-compatible, Pentium-based computer with a color monitor, 32MB (preferably 64MB) of RAM, at least 500MB

Chapter One
Required Equipment and Suppliers

(preferably 2GB) of free hard disk space, and Windows 95 installed is required.

The Lamination Pouches

Simple lamination pouches, suitable for non-critical ID, are available at local office supply stores. The problem is that many modern ID cards are made with magnetic-stripped PVC cards that can only be printed on with dye-sublimation card printers (they start at about $2,500). Paper laminated between simple lamination pouches will not fool anyone.

Teslin is the answer. It is a 7-millimeter, synthetic, paper-like, plastic card that can be printed on with an ink-jet printer. During the lamination process, it bonds to the pouches. The net effect is that the laminated card looks and feels like a PVC card.

This supplier sells lamination pouches of various thicknesses, with or without magnetic strips on the back, and Teslin. There may be others but the address/phone number of one verified source is:

POLAFIX INC.
PO Box 487
Drums, PA 18222
Phone: (717) 788-8800
Fax: (717) 788-4400
Order hotline: (800) 784-5678
Web site: http://www.polafix.com

Note: This is a legitimate company. If asked, pretend that the supplies are required for manufacturing employee IDs.

The Small Stuff

The following items are also required:
- an Exacto knife
- a metal ruler
- 600-grit sand paper
- large poster board closely matching the ID photograph's background color
- photo-quality glossy paper
- Elmer's Mucilage glue

Chapter Two
Configuring Photoshop

This chapter discusses the required Photoshop configuration. To successfully use this book, it is imperative that Photoshop is configured as follows.

How to Make Driver's Licenses and Other ID
on Your Home Computer

12

Step 1
   Start Photoshop.

Step 2
   Select *File* from the menu bar. Select *Preferences* from the pull-down menu. Select *General*. Confirm that the General Properties window is configured as follows:

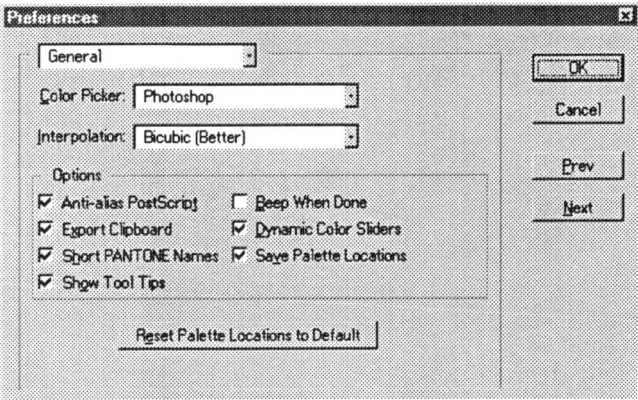

Chapter Two
Configuring Photoshop

Step 3

Select *Display & Cursors* from the Preferences pick box. Confirm that the Display & Cursors Properties window is configured as follows:

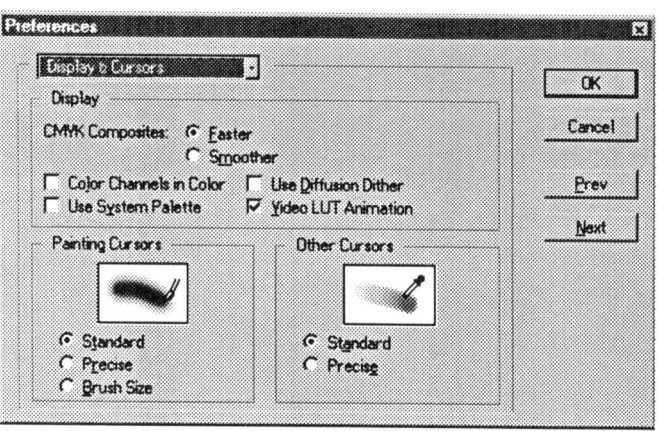

How to Make Driver's Licenses and Other ID on Your Home Computer

14

Step 4
Select *Transparency & Gamut* from the Preferences pick box. Confirm that the Display & Cursors Properties window is configured as follows:

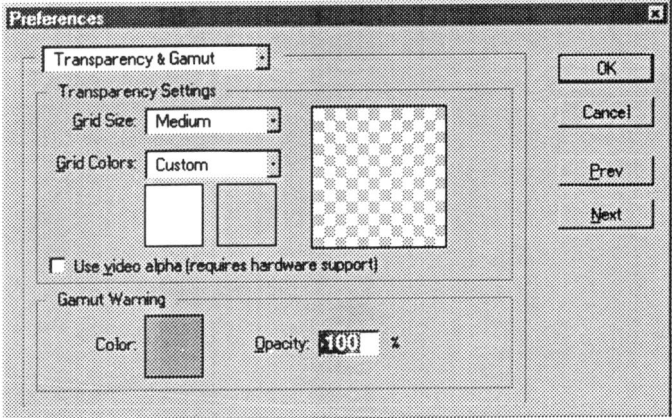

Chapter Two
Configuring Photoshop

15

Step 5

Select *Units & Rulers* from the Preferences pick box. Confirm that the Display & Cursors Properties window is configured as follows:

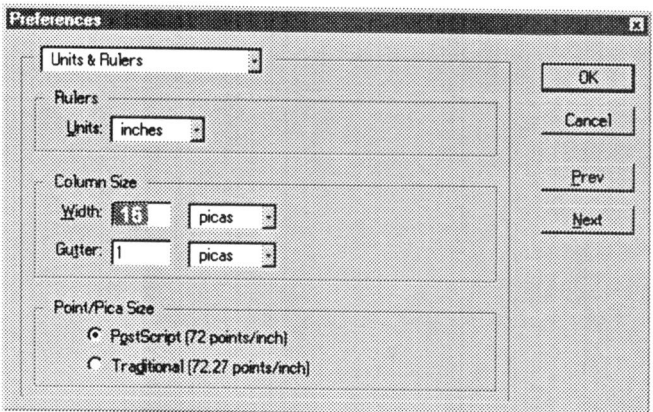

How to Make Driver's Licenses and Other ID
on Your Home Computer

16

Step 6

Select *Memory & Image Cache* from the Preferences pick box. Confirm that the Display & Cursors Properties window is configured as follows:

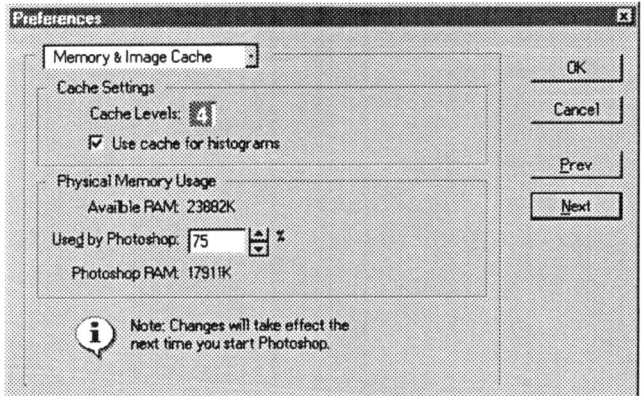

Chapter Two
Configuring Photoshop

17

Step 7
Select *Guides & Grid* from the Preferences pick box. Confirm that the Display & Cursors Properties window is configured as follows:

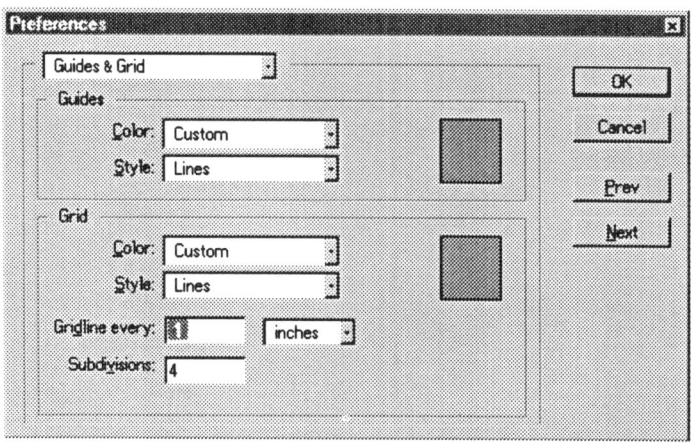

Chapter Three
Acquiring the License Template

This chapter discusses three ways to acquire a license template.

Acquisition

The first thing required is a good image of the license to be manufactured. It will need to be from a state at least 500 miles away. The reason is simple: People will recognize that it's a valid ID, but they won't be overly familiar with its appearance. They'll be far more likely to accept it.

NEW JERSEY

Don't waste time counterfeiting a New Jersey ID. It has been so heavily counterfeited over the past few years that it is known from coast to coast as a problem ID. This reputation means that all New Jersey IDs come under increased scrutiny. In fact, it has gotten so bad, that even if the presented New Jersey ID is perfect, it may be refused.

There are several ways to obtain a good driver's license image:

Option 1: Scan a friend's out-of-state license. The obvious disadvantage here is that the friend will ask a lot of questions. Personally, I tell no one of my activities. One never knows when someone, even a trusted friend, will inadvertently say something to the wrong person. So unless he's a very good friend (or a very sound sleeper), use this technique sparingly. Chapter Four provides step-by-step instructions for creating a license template from a physical license. If you happen to find a lost wallet in the street, you can use the driver's license as a template. Just return the rest of the items to the owner.

Option 2: Log on to the Internet. There are many people on the Web interested in trading license images. Chapter Five provides step-by-step instructions for finding and trading license templates on the Internet.

Option 3: Create the license template using Photoshop. License templates are surprisingly easy to create. Many licenses are simply a series of bars and boxes. State seals and other identifying markings are available all over the Internet. It only takes a small amount of artistic ability and about ten hours to easily create a license template.

Chapter Three
Acquiring the License Template

A VERY USEFUL GUIDE

The ID Checking Guide contains images of all US driver's licenses and is very useful in identifying licenses which are easy to manufacture. It also contains detailed information on the codes that are included on almost every license.

There are several places to obtain this on the Internet. One source is http://www.webbanker.com/pub2.html, or write the company directly. The address is:

Driver's License Guide Company
PO Box 5303
Redwood City, CA 94063

The company is a bit self-righteous so come up with a cover story. Write the company on letterhead that identifies you as a bar or restaurant. Change your answering machine message to match the letterhead, because you may get a call.

Chapter Four
Scanning the License and Preparing the License Template

This chapter provides step-by-step instructions for creating a license template from a physical license (Option 1 in Chapter Three).

Required Materials

Photo-quality glossy paper is required for the completion of this chapter.

Part One:
Scanning the License

Step 1A
Clean the license thoroughly with glass cleaner. The license should look like new prior to scanning.

Step 1B
Clean the scanner's glass thoroughly.

Step 1C
Using the software that came with the scanner, scan the front and back of the license at the maximum (software-enhanced) resolution.* All scanners have software extrapolation which allows them to produce

How to Make Driver's Licenses and Other ID on Your Home Computer

much more detailed scans than their optical limitations would suggest. Save the image as a *.JPG* file.

Note: If a "Lack of Memory" error occurs, reduce the scan resolution. Do not reduce the resolution to less than 1200 DPI or the scan quality will suffer.

Step 1D
After scanning and saving the image, load it into Photoshop by pressing the *CONTROL* and *O* keys simultaneously and selecting the file saved in Step 1C.

Step 1E
Select *Image* from the menu bar. Select *Image Size* from the pull-down menu. Enter a *Resolution* of 1200 (pixels/inch) in the *Print Size* box. At this point, the license template will appear to be enormous. Don't worry, it's just Photoshop's way of showing the increased detail requested.

Step 1F
Press the *SHIFT* and *CONTROL* and *P* keys simultaneously. Select *Properties*. Configure the printer to print on photo-quality glossy paper at the maximum printer resolution. This will vary based on the printer so it will not be covered here — consult the printer's owner's manual.

Step 1G
Load the printer with photo-quality glossy paper. Press the *CONTROL* and *P* keys simultaneously. Click on the *OK* button. This will print the license template.

Chapter Four
Scanning the License and Preparing the License Template

Note: It is important to print the image prior to comparing it to the physical license. If the physical license is compared to the image on the display, any deficiencies or biases in the printer or monitor will not be taken into consideration.

BE SMART!
Printing a counterfeit license is illegal. Burn all unused printouts.

Step 1H
Compare the printout to the physical license. Pay careful attention to the state seal, the crispness of the characters, and the correctness of the colors.

Step 1I
Now it's time to fix any imperfections in the scanned/printed image. The following is a list of potential problems and the ways to correct them:

A. *Colors Slightly Incorrect.* Sometimes scanned images appear slightly off color. Photoshop allows the license template's color balance to be adjusted. Press the *CONTROL* and *B* keys simultaneously. The *Color Balance* window will pop up. Make sure the *Preview* box is checked. The license template's reds, blues, and greens in the shadows, midtones and highlights can now be independently adjusted. Slide the adjustment sliders and see how they impact the license template. After a few adjustments, the license template image will look perfect. Return to Step 1G.

B. The Scan Picked Up License Imperfections or Scratches. Sometimes the scan amplifies license imperfections or makes the whites look a bit "dirty." Here's where Photoshop's Brightness/Contrast controls come into play. Select *Image* from the menu bar. Select *Adjust* from the pull-down menu. Select *Brightness/Contrast*. The *Brightness/Contrast* window will pop up. Make sure the *Preview* box is checked. Adjust the image via the adjustment sliders. Adding a touch of brightness and contrast will bring back the crisp whites and eliminate any scratches. Return to Step 1G.

C. Colors Way Off or Image Fuzzy. Be sure that the scanner and physical license are clean. Confirm that the scanner and printer are set for maximum resolution. Return to Step 1C.

D. Image Is at an Angle. Photoshop allows the angle of the image to be adjusted. Select *Image* from the menu bar. Press the *CONTROL* and " keys simultaneously to display a grid. Select *Rotate Canvas* from the pull-down menu. Select *Arbitrary*. Enter the angle that will make the image perfectly level. You'll probably miss on the first try but try it a few more times and eventually the image will be perfectly level. Don't bother printing out the image. It's pretty easy to judge the image's level right on the display screen.

Step 1J

Now it's time to trim the license. Confirm that the Tool Window is showing. If not, select *Window* from the menu

*Chapter Four
Scanning the License and Preparing
the License Template*

bar. Select *Show Tools* from the pull-down menu. The Tool Window will be displayed. Select the *Marquee Tool* from the Tool Window (it's the dashed box in the top left corner of the Tool Window). Click and drag the marquee line from the top left corner of the license to the lower right corner. Make sure that the resulting marquee box is as close to the license's edge as possible; if necessary, zoom in by pressing the *CONTROL* and *+* keys simultaneously. Press the *CONTROL* and *X* keys simultaneously to make the cut. Press the *CONTROL* and *N* keys simultaneously for a new window. Press the *CONTROL* and *V* keys simultaneously to paste the image in a new window. Close the old window without saving the now valueless image.

Step 1K
Carefully measure the height and width of the physical license.* Select *Image* from the menu bar. Select *Image Size* from the pull-down menu. After ensuring that the Constrain Proportions box is selected, enter the *Width* of the physical ID in the *Print Size* box. Photoshop will automatically calculate the height of the image and put the value in the *Height* section of the *Print Size* box. Make sure that Photoshop's calculation and the physical measurement of the IDs height are within 0.1 inches of each other — the closer the better.

***Note:** If the physical license is not available, simply measure the license template.

Step 1L
Save the image by simultaneously pressing the *SHIFT* and *CONTROL* and *S* keys. Be sure to save it as a

How to Make Driver's Licenses and Other ID on Your Home Computer

Photoshop file (by selecting *Photoshop (*.PSD, *.PDD)* from the *Save As* pick box). This will save all of the formatting information. While this is not particularly critical here, it will be in subsequent chapters.

FILE ENCRYPTION?

Consider encrypting all ID-related files. It will prevent a relative or, worse yet, a law-enforcement official from seeing the suspicious files. There are a number of very effective programs out there.

- JAWS TECHNOLOGIES L5 encryption software is absolutely unbreakable (4096 bit) and reasonably priced. A free 30-day trial is available. The Web site is http://www.jawstech.com.

- Pretty Good Privacy (PGP) is also a good choice. It is not as strong as JAWS L5, but it's free. It is available at http://web.mit.edu/network/pgp.html.

Chapter Four
Scanning the License and Preparing
the License Template

Part Two: Preparing the License Template

Step 2A

Now it's time to remove extraneous information, including all personal text and the signature block, from the license. Do not remove any generic text — it is a part of the license template and must remain.

DECISION POINT

Does the license contain an anti-counterfeiting image behind the text? If no, proceed to Step 2H. If yes, proceed to Step 2B.

Step 2B

Before continuing, the anti-counterfeiting image and the text that rests on top of it will need to be removed.

Set Photoshop's background color to the color of the license's background by clicking on the background swatch on the Tool Window then clicking on a blank portion of the license.

Select the *Marquee Tool* from the Tool Window (it's the dashed box in the top left corner of the Tool Window). Click and drag the marquee line from the top left corner to the lower right corner of the license area containing personal information. When all text information and anti-counterfeiting images are within the marquee line, press the *CONTROL* and *X* keys simultaneously to make the cut.

How to Make Driver's Licenses and Other ID on Your Home Computer

> **DECISION POINT**
>
> Was the anti-counterfeiting image deleted in Step 2B a hologram or a ghost image of the license's primary picture? If yes, its replacement will be described in subsequent chapters — proceed to Step 2H. If no, proceed to Step 2C.

Step 2C
Now the anti-counterfeiting image needs to be replaced. This book will assume that the image is a state seal.* State seals are all over the Internet. To find them:
- Log on to the Internet.
- Go to http://www.hotbot.com.
- Search for "image and state seals."

Note: If the image is not a state seal, use the techniques discussed here to find and replace the image.

Step 2D
Load the state seal image into Photoshop. Assess the picture using the techniques discussed earlier in this chapter, Step 1I.

Step 2E
Carefully measure the height of the state seal on the physical license.* Select *Image* from the menu bar. Select *Image Size* from the pull-down menu. Enter a *Resolution* of 1200 (pixels/inch) in the *Print Size* box. After ensuring that the Constrain Proportions box is selected, enter the *Width* of the state seal into the *Print Size* box. Photoshop will automatically calculate the

*Chapter Four
Scanning the License and Preparing
the License Template*

height of the image and put the value in the *Height* section of the *Print Size* box. Make sure that Photoshop's calculation and the physical measurement of the state seal's height are within 0.1 inches of each other — the closer the better.

Note: If the physical license is not available, measure the license template.

Step 2F
Confirm that the Tool Window is showing. If not, select *Window* from the menu bar. Select *Show Tools* from the pull-down menu. The Tool Window will be displayed. Select the *Marquee Tool* from the Tool Window (it's the dashed box in the top left corner of the Tool Window). Click and drag the marquee line from the state seal's top left corner to the lower right corner. Press the *CONTROL* and *X* keys simultaneously to make the cut.

Step 2G
Load the license template into Photoshop. Select *Layer* from the menu bar. Select *New* from the pull-down menu. Select *Layer.* Click on the *OK* button. Press the *CONTROL* and *V* keys simultaneously. The state seal will be pasted on a new layer of the license. Use the mouse to move the new image to the correct position.

DECISION POINT

Is the state seal the correct size? If no, repeat Steps 2C through 2G. If yes, proceed to Chapter Six.

How to Make Driver's Licenses and Other ID on Your Home Computer

Step 2H

Zoom in on the license by pressing the *CONTROL* and *+* keys simultaneously. Confirm that the Tool Window is showing. If not, select *Window* from the menu bar. Select *Show Tools* from the pull-down menu. The Tool Window will be displayed.

Set Photoshop's background color to the color of the license's background by clicking on the background swatch on the Tool Window then clicking on a blank portion of the license.

Select the *Marquee Tool* from the Tool Window (it's the dashed box in the top left corner of the Tool Window). Identify a small, blank portion of the license — no text, no seals, no nothing. Click and drag the marquee line from the top left corner to the lower right corner of the blank portion of the license template. Press the *CONTROL* and *X* keys simultaneously to make the cut.

Load the printer with photo-quality paper. Press the *CONTROL* and *P* keys simultaneously. Click on the *OK* button. This will print the license.

DECISION POINT

Closely examine the area of the test cut. Is it visible? If not, then proceed to step 2N. If so, then proceed to step 2I.

Step 2I

The cut is visible because the license's background color is not consistent. Never fear — there is an easy answer — it's called masking. Instead of cutting the text

*Chapter Four
Scanning the License and Preparing
the License Template*

out of the license, masking will cover the text by pasting a piece of blank license over it. This method solves the problems caused by inconsistent license background colors.

Step 2J
Using the *Marquee Tool* (from the Tool Window), select a small blank portion of the license — it should be just a little bit larger than the license font and approximately a quarter of an inch long. Press the *CONTROL* and *C* keys simultaneously. This copies the mask.

Step 2K
Press the *CONTROL* and *V* keys simultaneously. This will paste the mask directly over the area copied in Step 2J. Select the *Move Tool* from the Tool Window (it's the top right box on the Tool Window). With the mouse, move the mask over the personal text to be removed. Notice that the text below the mask is obscured.

Step 2L
Repeat Step 2K until all personal text is obscured.

Step 2M
Press the *SHIFT* and *CONTROL* and *E* keys to merge all layers. Proceed to Step 2O.

Step 2N
Continue to cut personal text via the *Marquee Tool* (as described in Step 2H) until all personal text is removed.

Step 20

Save the image by simultaneously pressing the *SHIFT* and *CONTROL* and *S* keys. Be sure to save it as a Photoshop file by selecting *Photoshop (*.PSD, *.PDD)* from the *Save As* pick box. This will save all of the formatting information.

ALWAYS USE UNIQUE FILE NAMES

When saving the file, always use a unique file name. If something goes wrong in subsequent steps, this will allow the retrieval of previously saved images.

A suggested format is "ChapterX-StepY.psd" (which in this case would translate to *"Chapterfour-Step20.psd"*).

Chapter Five
Getting a License Template on the Internet

Chapter Five
Getting a License Template on the Internet

This chapter provides step-by-step instructions for finding and trading license templates on the Internet (Option 2 in Chapter Three).

PROCEED WITH CAUTION

1. Before transmitting the license to a stranger with potentially bad intentions, make sure that all critical information is removed.
2. Transmitting a license scan over the Internet is a highly suspicious (and probably illegal) activity. Do not expose your true identity or ISP-based e-mail address during the exchange.

Step 1
- Log on to the Internet.
- Go to http://www.hotmail.com and set up a free anonymous e-mail address.
- Go to http://www.xoom.com and set up a free anonymous 11 MEG Web site account. This will allow the exchange of template files up to 11 MEGS. Hotmail is limited to 2 MEGS (this is rarely large enough).

Step 2
To find message boards for people interested in exchanging fake ID scans:
- Log on to the Internet.
- Go to http://www.hotbot.com.
- Search for "Fake ID and message board" or "Fake ID and messages."
- Follow the links to the identified sites.

Step 3
Post a message like this:

<<I have a perfect scan of a Florida license (front and back, 1200 x 1200 DPI). Will trade for any other state (front and back, 1200 x 1200 DPI, or better) except New Jersey. Contact me at *(YOURUSERNAME)*@hotmail.com>>.

Step 4
After someone contacts you, write him the following note:

<<Hey *(NAME)*,
I'd like to exchange the templates using my XOOM account. That way we can transmit large files. I ZIPPED and password-protected my file, then FTP'd it to FTP.XOOM.COM. The filename is (*FILENAME*).

After you download it, delete it from XOOM.COM. After you delete it, ZIP and password-protect your file and FTP it to FTP.XOOM.COM. After we both have the files, we'll exchange passwords.

Chapter Five
Getting a License Template on the Internet

The XOOM username is *(USERNAME)*. The XOOM password is *(PASSWORD)*.
Thanks. >>

Step 5
After your contact uploads his license template file to the XOOM account, download it and save it on the hard drive.

Step 6
After downloading the file, send him a note with the ZIP password.

Step 7
Change the XOOM account's password.

Step 8
After receiving the ZIP file password, decompress the ZIP file.

Chapter Six
Adding the Picture

Chapter Six
Adding the Picture

This chapter provides step-by-step instructions on taking the picture, sizing and trimming it and placing the picture on the license template. It assumes that you have a camera with a timer.

Required Materials

The following materials are required for the completion of this chapter:
- photo-quality glossy paper
- metal-edged ruler
- poster board that matches the license photograph's background color

Step 1
Examine the photograph on the ID. Take note of the:
- background color
- position of the camera (typically at eye level)
- photo composition (typically the picture is from the top of the head to the bottom of the neck)

Recreate the photograph's conditions as closely as possible. Obtain a large poster board closely matching the license photograph's background color. Secure it to the wall at head and shoulder level. For best results, use

How to Make Driver's Licenses and Other ID on Your Home Computer

a couple of 500-watt halogen shop lamps to illuminate the poster board (they cost about $8 each at the local hardware store). Be sure to position them to the left and right of the poster board, pointing directly at the subject. This will minimize shadowing. If halogen shop lamps are not available, use the camera's flash. Be sure to use the anti-red-eye setting.

Use a tripod (or anything stable) to raise the camera to the appropriate level. For best results, fill the entire frame area with your head and shoulders.

Now set the camera's timer, stand in front of the poster board and take several pictures of yourself.

Step 2
Scan or load the pictures into the computer using the software that came with the scanner or digital camera. Examine the pictures and choose the one that most closely resembles the composition of the physical license's picture. Pay careful attention to the background color: It should be identical or as close as possible to the background color on the ID template.

Step 3
Load the picture into Photoshop. Assess the picture using the techniques discussed in Chapter Four, Step 1l.

Step 4
Select *Image* from the menu bar. Select *Image Size* from the pull-down menu. Enter a *Resolution* of 1200 (pixels/inch) in the *Print Size* box.

Chapter Six
Adding the Picture

41

Step 5

Now it's time to trim the picture. Confirm that the horizontal and vertical rulers are displayed on your picture. If not, press the *CONTROL* and *R* keys simultaneously.

Confirm that the Tool Window is showing. If not, select *Window* from the menu bar. Select *Show Tools* from the pull-down menu. The Tool Window will be displayed. Select the *Marquee Tool* from the Tool Window (it's the dashed box in the top left corner of the Tool Window). Identify the portion of the picture to be cut. Click and drag the marquee line from the top left corner to the lower right corner. Use the rulers to ensure that the area of the picture is the exact size* of the picture on the physical license. (If the physical license is not available, measure the license template.) Be sure to center the head and shoulders as closely as possible to their position on the physical license. Press the *CONTROL* and *X* keys simultaneously to make the cut.

Note: If it is not possible to select the desired image and maintain the desired size (i.e., the picture is too large or too small), adjust the overall image size using the method discussed in Chapter Four, Step 1K.

Step 6

Press the *CONTROL* and *N* keys simultaneously for a new window. Press the *CONTROL* and *V* keys simultaneously to paste the picture image in a new window. Save the image by simultaneously pressing the *SHIFT* and *CONTROL* and *S* keys. Be sure to save it as a Photoshop file (by selecting *Photoshop (*.PSD, *.PDD)*

How to Make Driver's Licenses and Other ID on Your Home Computer

42

from the *Save As* pick box). Close the old window without saving the now valueless image.

Step 7
Now it's time to see if the picture is the correct size. Load the license template into Photoshop. Select *Layer* from the menu bar. Select *New* from the pull-down menu. Select *Layer*. Click on the *OK* button. Press the *CONTROL* and *V* keys simultaneously. The picture will be pasted on a new layer of the license. Use the mouse to move the new picture over the existing picture. If the picture does not fit perfectly over the existing picture, repeat steps 4 through 7, adjusting the size of the trimmed picture.

DECISION POINT

Does the new picture obscure any of the license's anti-counterfeiting measures (seals, signatures, etc.)? If no, then proceed to step 13. If yes, then proceed to step 8.

Step 8
Close the license template without saving. Load the picture file created in Step 6.

Step 9
The goal is to place the new picture onto the existing license template without obscuring existing anti-counterfeiting measures, such as state seals, camera numbers or overlapping the signature. To achieve this goal, the picture will need to be trimmed as depicted in the illustration on the next page.

Chapter Six
Adding the Picture

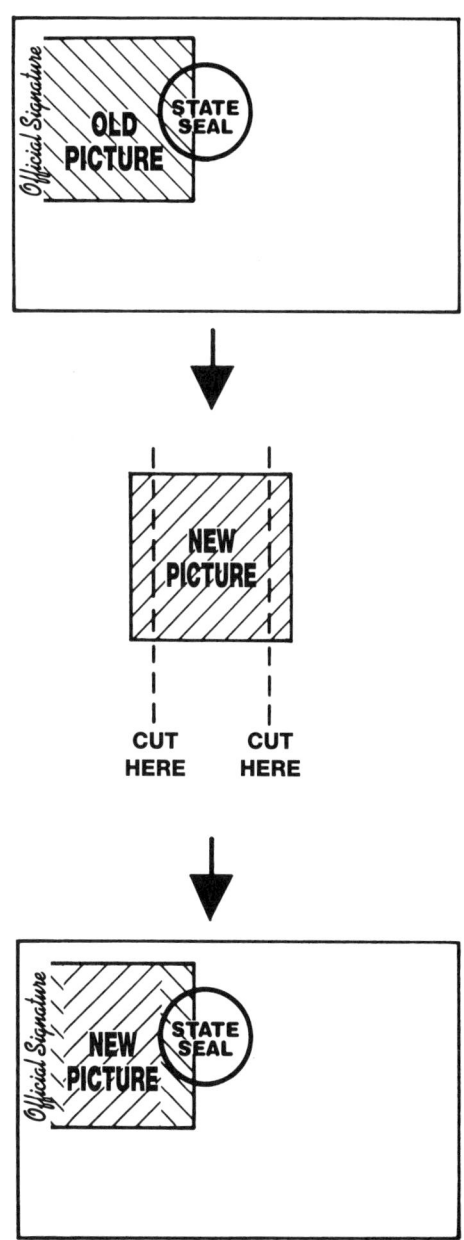

How to Make Driver's Licenses and Other ID on Your Home Computer

Step 10

Confirm that the Tool Window is showing. If not, select *Window* from the menu bar. Select *Show Tools* from the pull-down menu. The Tool Window will be displayed. Select the *Marquee Tool* from the Tool Window (it's the dashed box in the top left corner of the Tool Window). Identify the portion of the picture to be cut (use the illustration on the preceding page as a guide). Click and drag the marquee line from the top left corner to the lower right corner of the identified portion. Press the *CONTROL* and *X* keys simultaneously to make the cut.

Step 11

Load the license template into Photoshop. Select *Layer* from the menu bar. Select *New* from the pull-down menu. Select *Layer*. Click on the *OK* button. Press the *CONTROL* and *V* keys simultaneously. The new picture will be pasted on a new layer of the license template. Use the mouse to move the new picture over the existing picture. Be sure not to cover any of the anti-counterfeiting measures.

Step 12

Now it's time to eliminate the color difference between the new picture's background and the license template's old picture. Press the *CONTROL* and *B* keys simultaneously. The *Color Balance* window will pop up. Make sure the *Preview* box is checked. Adjust the new picture's reds, blues, and greens in the shadows, midtones, and highlights to make it perfectly match the license template's old picture.

Chapter Six
Adding the Picture

45

Step 13

Save the image by simultaneously pressing the *SHIFT* and *CONTROL* and *S* keys. Be sure to save it as a Photoshop file by selecting *Photoshop (*.PSD, *.PDD)* from the *Save As* pick box.

DECISION POINT

Does the license contain a "ghost-image" of the primary picture? If not, then proceed to Step 20. If so, then proceed to Step 14.

Step 14

Press the *CONTROL* and *N* keys simultaneously. Press the *CONTROL* and *V* keys simultaneously.

Step 15

Select *Image* from the menu bar. Select *Image Size* from the pull-down menu. Adjust the image size using the method discussed in Chapter Four, Step 1K.

Step 16

Press the *CONTROL* and *U* keys simultaneously. Confirm that the *Preview* box is checked. Use the *Lightness* slider to add light until the picture fades to the correct level. Click *OK*.

Step 17

Confirm that the Tool Window is showing. If not, select *Window* from the menu bar. Select *Show Tools* from the pull-down menu. The Tool Window will be displayed. Select the *Marquee Tool* from the Tool Window (it's the dashed box in the top left corner of the Tool Window).

How to Make Driver's Licenses and Other ID on Your Home Computer

Click and drag the marquee line from the image's top left corner to the lower right corner. Press the *CONTROL* and *X* keys simultaneously to make the cut.

Step 18
Load the license template image saved in Step 13 into Photoshop. Select *Layer* from the menu bar. Select *New* from the pull-down menu. Select *Layer*. Click on the *OK* button. Press the *CONTROL* and *V* keys simultaneously. The new picture will be pasted on a new layer of the license template. Use the mouse to move the new picture to the correct location.

Step 19
Save the image by simultaneously pressing the *SHIFT* and *CONTROL* and *S* keys. Be sure to save it as a Photoshop file by selecting *Photoshop (*.PSD, *.PDD)* from the *Save As* pick box.

Step 20
Load the printer with photo-quality paper. Select *File* from the menu bar. Select *Print* from the pull-down menu. Click on the *OK* button. This will print the license.

Step 21
Now it's time to assess the printout. The following is a list of common problems and the ways to correct them.

A. The Outline of the New Picture Is Visible. Return to Step 12 to re-adjust the color balance.

Chapter Six
Adding the Picture

47

B. One of the Anti-counterfeiting Measures Has Been Obscured.

DECISION POINT

Can the picture be trimmed further without chopping off anything conspicuous such as an ear, hair, or chin? If yes, then return to Step 9 and trim the picture more aggressively. If no, then the new picture's image size needs to be scaled down — return to Step 5.

C. Skin Tone Problems.
If the new picture's skin tones are way off, making the picture look suspect, there are two options:

Option 1: Press the *SHIFT* and *CONTROL* and *E* keys. This will merge all visible layers, integrating the new picture and the license template. Press the *CONTROL* and *B* keys simultaneously. The *Color Balance* window will pop up. Make sure the *Preview* box is checked. Adjust the integrated image's reds, blues, and greens in the shadows, midtones, and highlights to correct the skin tone problems.

DECISION POINT

Have the skin tone colors been corrected without adversely impacting the rest of the license template's colors? If yes, then return to step 14. If no, continue to Option 2.

Option 2: Acquire a background that more closely matches the color of the license template and return to Step 1.

Chapter Seven
License Font Identification

This chapter provides step-by-step instructions for license font creation and utilization.

Step 1

Select *Window* from the menu bar. Select *Show Tools* from the pull-down menu. The Tool Window will be displayed. Select the *Type Tool* from the Tool Window (it's the large T in the Tool Window).

DECISION POINT

Is there a license scan available that contains original personal information?
If yes, proceed to Step 2. If no, proceed to Step 9.

Step 2

Load a license scan that contains original personal information.

Step 3

Select *Image* from the menu bar. Select *Image Size* from the pull-down menu. Enter a *Resolution* of 1200 (pixels/inch) in the *Print Size* box.

How to Make Driver's Licenses and Other ID on Your Home Computer

Step 4

Select a word to attempt to duplicate. Adjust the image size (by zooming in or out) so that the chosen word fills about three-quarters of the screen. With the mouse, move the cursor to the appropriate location. Click the left mouse button. The *Type Tool* window will be displayed. Make sure that the *Font* box and *Size* box (on the bottom of the *Type Tool* window) are checked.

Step 5

Type in the chosen word. Use the *Font* pick box to select the font that matches the chosen word. Adjust the font size by entering integers in the *Size* window. When the created text matches the text chosen in Step 4, click the *OK* button.

Step 6

Select the *Move Tool* from the Tool Window (it's the top right box on the Tool Window). With the mouse, move the text created in Step 6 directly over the word chosen in Step 4.

Step 7

Now it's time to assess the text created in Step 6. The following is a list of potential problems and the ways to correct them.

- **A. *The Characters Are Too Big or Too Small.*** Select *Layer* from the menu bar. Select *Delete Layer* from the pull-down menu. This will delete the text created in Step 6. Return to Step 4. This time decrease or increase the font size, as necessary.

Chapter Seven
License Font Identification

51

B. The Spacing Between Characters Is Wrong. Select *Layer* from the menu bar. Select *Delete Layer* from the pull-down menu. This will delete the text created in Step 6. If the spacing is too wide, then return to Step 4 — this time enter a negative number in the *Spacing* field. If the spacing is too narrow, then return to Step 4 — this time enter a positive number in the *Spacing* field.

C. The Font Doesn't Match. Delete the text created in Step 6 by selecting *Layer* from the menu bar. Select *Delete Layer* from the pull-down menu.

DECISION POINT

Are there additional fonts available? If yes, return to Step 4 and try the other fonts. If no, proceed to Step 8.

Step 8
If there are no Photoshop standard fonts that match the license, there are several options:

Option 1: Get More Fonts: CDs with 2000 fonts are available for about $5 at most office supply stores. If this option is selected, install the fonts, then return to Step 4.

Option 2: Use Similar Fonts: Use the closest font available. It is unlikely that the average person will notice the difference — especially since the out-of-state license will not be particularly familiar to him. If this option is utilized, be sure to replace all license parameters. Different font faces on the same license will be very obvious to the most casual observer. If this option is selected, proceed to Chapter 8.

Option 3: Create the Font: There is a public-domain program on the Web called Softy. It allows the user to open up an existing font and modify the characters. Softy is a great program that makes this process quite easy. This option works particularly well if a Photoshop standard font comes very close to matching the license's font but needs slight modification. If this option is selected, proceed to Chapter Eight.

Step 9
If there is not a license scan available that contains original personal information, then another source of information is required. Consult *The ID Checking Guide* (profiled in Chapter Four). It contains images of all US driver's licenses.

Chapter Eight
License Personalization

This chapter provides step-by-step instructions for adding new information to the license template.

Required Materials

The following materials are required for the completion of this chapter:
- photo-quality glossy paper
- a metal-edged ruler

Part One:
The Text

Step 1A

Examine the front of the license. Typically, licenses include the following details:

Name	**Issue date**
Address	**License expiration**
Height	**License number**
Weight	**Class**
Eyes	**Restrictions**
Sex	**Signature block**
Birthdate	

How to Make Driver's Licenses and Other ID on Your Home Computer

Step 1B

Load the license template. Confirm that the Tool Window is showing. If not, select *Window* from the menu bar. Select *Show Tools* from the pull-down menu. The Tool Window will be displayed. Select the *Type Tool* from the Tool Window (it's the large T in the Tool Window).

LOOKING FOR A VALID STREET ADDRESS IN A DIFFERENT STATE?

Start at the US Postal Service's City/State/Zip Code Associations Web page at http://www.usps.com/ncsc. Enter the desired city and state and this page provides the zip code.

Continue to Yahoo's mapping Web page at http://maps.yahoo.com. Enter a typical street address, like 14 Elm Street (well, maybe not that obvious). If Yahoo maps it, then it's valid — use it.

Step 1C

With the mouse, move the cursor to the appropriate location. Click the left mouse button. Select the appropriate font, font size, and alignment (from Chapter Seven) in the *Type Tool* box. Type the desired text in the text box. Click *OK.*

BE TRULY ANONYMOUS

When creating licenses, amateurs tend to use their own name on the counterfeited license — this way they'll have back-up ID. True anonymity can be a powerful tool. Don't reduce the utility of the counterfeited license by using any information that may reveal your true identity. Creating back-up ID will be discussed in subsequent chapters.

Chapter Eight
License Personalization

55

Step 1D

Select the *Move Tool* from the Tool Window (it's the top right box on the Tool Window). With the mouse, move the text to the appropriate location.

Step 1E

Repeat Steps 1C and 1D until all the desired text is entered. Be sure to use the same spacing, number of characters/numbers and codes as on the original license.

Step 1F

Save the image by simultaneously pressing the *SHIFT* and *CONTROL* and *S* keys. Be sure to save it as a Photoshop file by selecting *Photoshop (*.PSD, *.PDD)* from the *Save As* pick box.

Part Two:
The Signature Block

Step 2A

Measure the height and width of the signature block on the physical license or license template. Multiply the height and width of the signature block by four. Draw a rectangle on a white sheet of paper with the multiplied dimensions. Use a black pen to write your signature in the signature block.

Step 2B

Scan or load the signature into the computer using the software that came with the scanner, using the

How to Make Driver's Licenses and Other ID on Your Home Computer

techniques discussed in Chapter Four. Save the image as a *.JPG* file.

Step 2C
Load the signature scan into Photoshop. This is a pretty easy scan so there shouldn't be any problems. If there are, return to Step 2B.

Step 2D
Confirm that the Tool Window is showing. If not, select *Window* from the menu bar. Select *Show Tools* from the pull-down menu. The Tool Window will be displayed. Select the *Marquee Tool* from the Tool Window (it's the dashed box in the top left corner of the Tool Window). Click and drag the marquee line from the top left corner to the lower right corner of the signature block. Press the *CONTROL* and *X* keys simultaneously to make the cut.

Step 2E
Press the *CONTROL* and *N* keys simultaneously. A new window will pop up. Make sure that the *TRANSPARENT* box is checked. Click *OK*.

Step 2F
Press the *CONTROL* and *V* keys simultaneously to paste the image in the new window.

Step 2G
Select the *Magic Wand Tool* from the Tool Window. Click the cursor on the signature image. Photoshop will find the edges of the signature image and outline them with a dashed line. Press the *CONTROL* and *X* keys to cut the background away from the signature image.

Chapter Eight
License Personalization

Step 2H

Continue to click the magic wand on the signature and cut the background away until all the colored background is deleted and the signature sits on a transparent background. Zoom in on various parts of the signature by pressing the *CONTROL* and + keys simultaneously. Reconfirm that all of the original background has been deleted.

Step 2I

Select *Image* from the menu bar. Select *Image Size* from the pull-down menu. After ensuring that the Constrain Proportions box is selected, enter the *Width* of the physical IDs signature block into the *Print Size* box. Photoshop will automatically calculate the height of the image and put the value in the *Width* section of the *Print Size* box. Make sure that Photoshop's calculation and the physical measurement of the IDs height are within 0.1 inches of each other — the closer the better.

Step 2J

Select the *Marquee Tool* from the Tool Window (it's the dashed box in the top left corner of the Tool Window). Click and drag the marquee line from the top left corner to the lower right corner of the signature block. Press the *CONTROL* and *X* keys simultaneously to make the cut.

Step 2K

Load the license template into Photoshop. Press the *CONTROL* and *V* keys simultaneously. This will paste the signature on the license template.

How to Make Driver's Licenses and Other ID on Your Home Computer

Step 2L
Select the *Move Tool* from the Tool Window (it's the top right box on the Tool Window). With the mouse, move the signature block to the appropriate location.

Step 2M
Save the image by simultaneously pressing the *SHIFT* and *CONTROL* and *S* keys. Be sure to save it as a Photoshop file by selecting *Photoshop (*.PSD, *.PDD)* from the *Save As* pick box. Close the old window without saving the now valueless image.

Chapter Nine
Holograms

This chapter discusses several options for dealing with holograms.

Option 1: Leave the Hologram Off: Unless you are underaged and trying to get into a bar, out-of-state IDs are usually just as effective without the hologram. People just don't know what the out-of-state ID is supposed to look like. If the ID looks legitimate, with or without a hologram, it is very likely to be accepted.

Option 2: Purchase a Hologram: An official-looking eagle-seal hologram can be purchased at http://www.nic-inc.com for a couple of dollars. No, it's not the seal that's supposed to be on the ID but it is a very good-looking hologram and will add an air of legitimacy to the ID.

Option 3: Take the Hologram From a Real ID: If you have the good fortune of possessing an official version of the ID you are counterfeiting, the following method is often effective:

How to Make Driver's Licenses and Other ID on Your Home Computer

- Buy some acetone at any hardware store.
- Pour the acetone into a small container and place the real ID into it. (The acetone eats the glue away allowing the ID to separate easily.)
- Peel the hologram off the real license and place it on the fake license.

Note: This method will obviously destroy the real ID.

Option 4: ALPS MD-Series Printers: ALPS manufactures printers that are capable of printing in blue, magenta, silver and gold metallic ink. The MD-1300 costs about $350 and is quite capable of printing a passable simulated hologram.

Chapter Ten
License Structure

Before proceeding to license printing, cutting and laminating, it is important to understand the three types of license structures. Each structure is treated differently in subsequent chapters.

Structure One — Simple Lamination: In Structure One, the information card is surrounded by a lamination pouch. Chapter Eleven provides detailed instructions for printing, cutting and laminating a "Structure One" license.

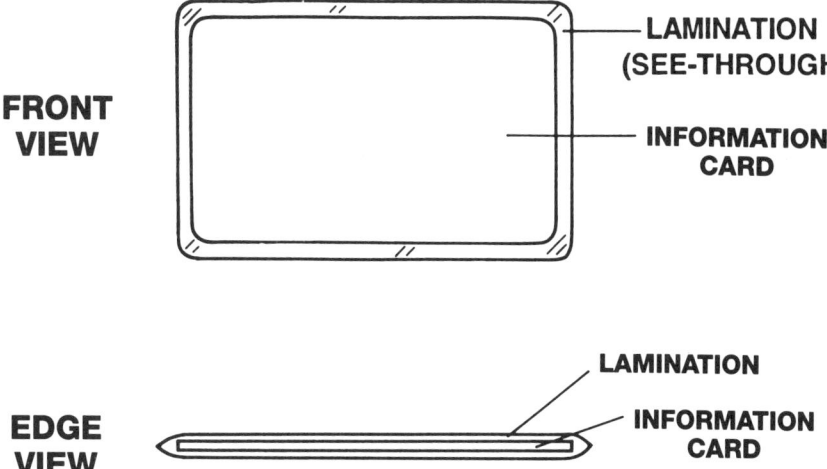

How to Make Driver's Licenses and Other ID on Your Home Computer

Structure Two — PVC Card Overlay: In Structure Two, the information card is glued onto the PVC card backing. The front of the license is covered with a lamination layer. Chapter Twelve provides detailed instructions for printing, cutting and laminating a "Structure Two" license.

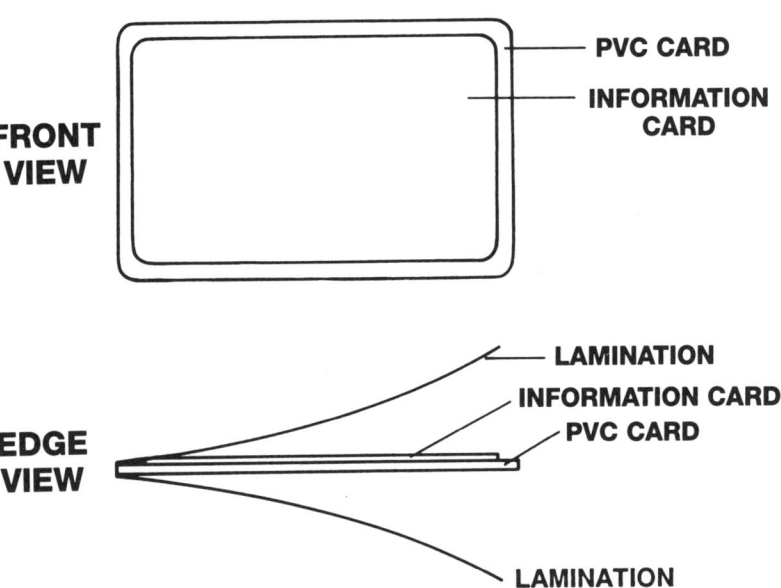

Chapter Ten
License Structure

63

Structure Three — Rigid Plastic Card License: In Structure Three, information is printed via a dye sublimation printer on a PVC card. The front of the license is covered with a lamination layer. Chapter Thirteen provides detailed instructions for printing, cutting and laminating a "Structure Three" license.

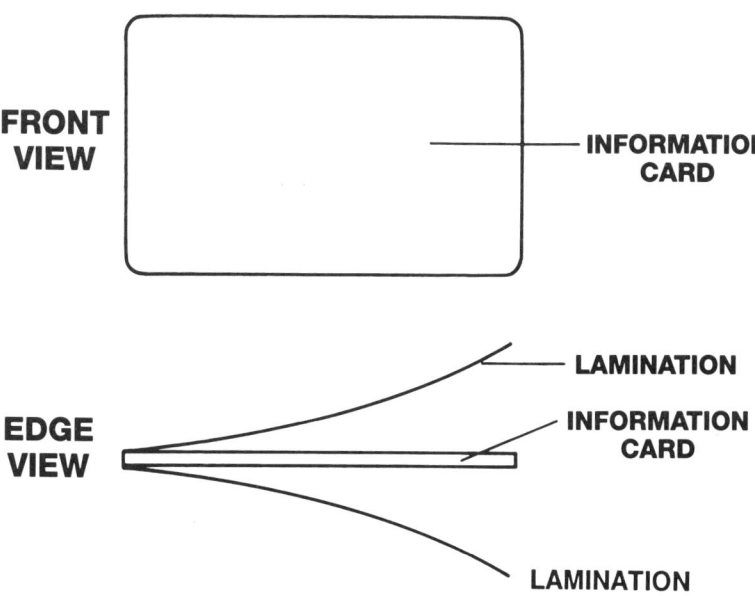

*Chapter Eleven
Printing, Cutting, and Laminating
Structure One Licenses*

Chapter Eleven
Printing, Cutting, and Laminating Structure One Licenses

This chapter provides step-by-step instructions for completing the Structure One license.

Required Materials

The following materials are required for the completion of this chapter:

- a 10-millimeter lamination pouch (with or without a magnetic strip)
- a Teslin card
- card laminator
- photo-quality paper
- Elmer's Mucilage glue
- an Exacto knife, cutting board, and metal-edged ruler
- 600-grit sandpaper
- any credit card or phone card with rounded edges

How to Make Driver's Licenses and Other ID on Your Home Computer

66

Step 1
   Load the front and back of the license template into Photoshop.

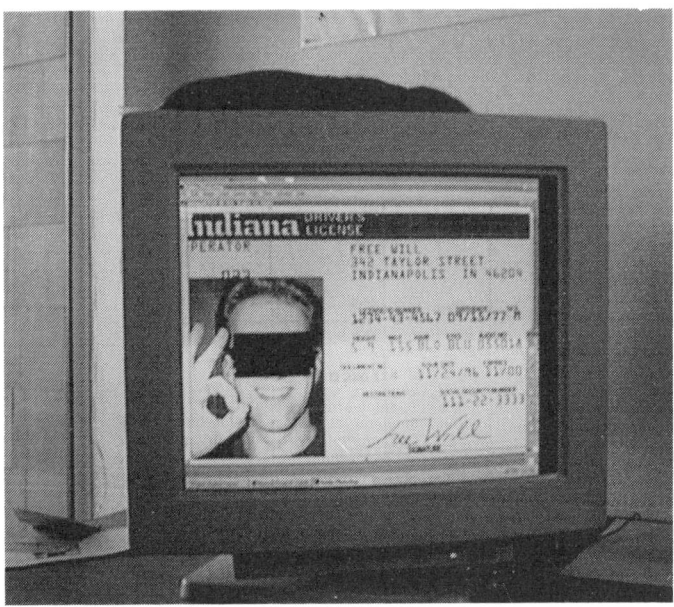

Chapter Eleven
Printing, Cutting, and Laminating
Structure One Licenses

Step 2
Select *Image* from the menu bar. Select *Image Size* from the pull-down menu. Confirm that the *Resolution* is set to 1200 (pixels/inch).

Step 3
Press the *SHIFT* and *CONTROL* and *P* keys simultaneously. Select *Properties*. (This will vary based on the printer so it will not be covered here — consult the printer's owner's manual.)

Step 4
Load the printer with photo-quality paper. Press the *CONTROL* and *P* keys simultaneously. Click on the *OK* button. This will print the license.

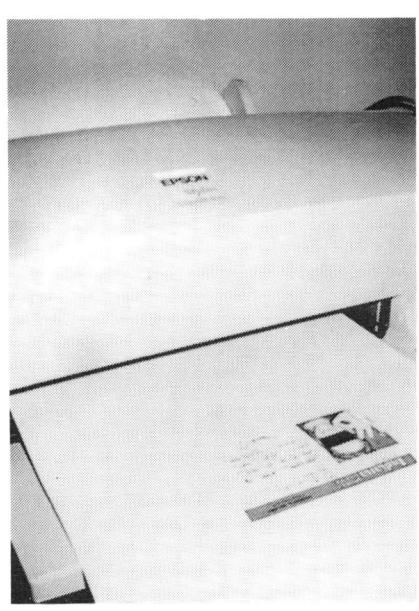

How to Make Driver's Licenses and Other ID
on Your Home Computer

Step 5

Although the license printout should be perfect at this point, quickly check the quality as discussed in Chapter Four, Step 1l.

Step 6

Lay the license printout on the cutting board. Use the ruler and the Exacto knife to cut out the front and back of the license. The rounded corners of a credit card or phone card can be used as an aid for cutting the rounded corners.

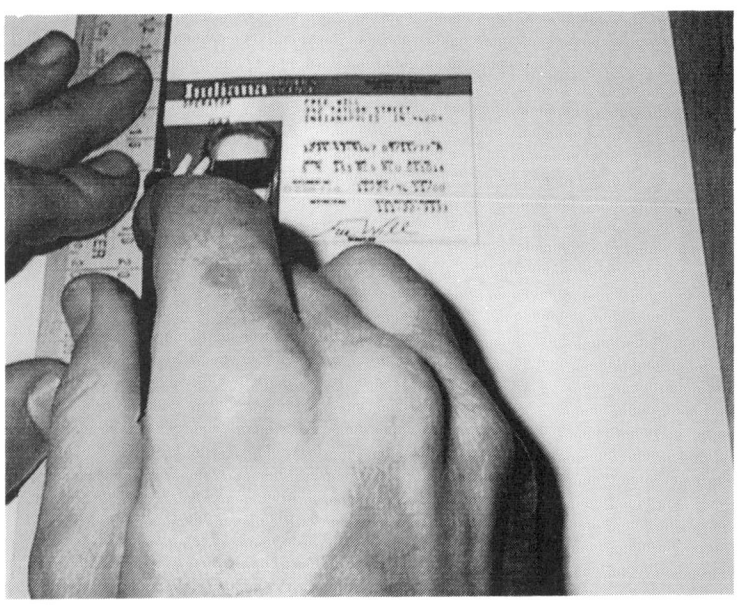

*Chapter Eleven
Printing, Cutting, and Laminating
Structure One Licenses
69*

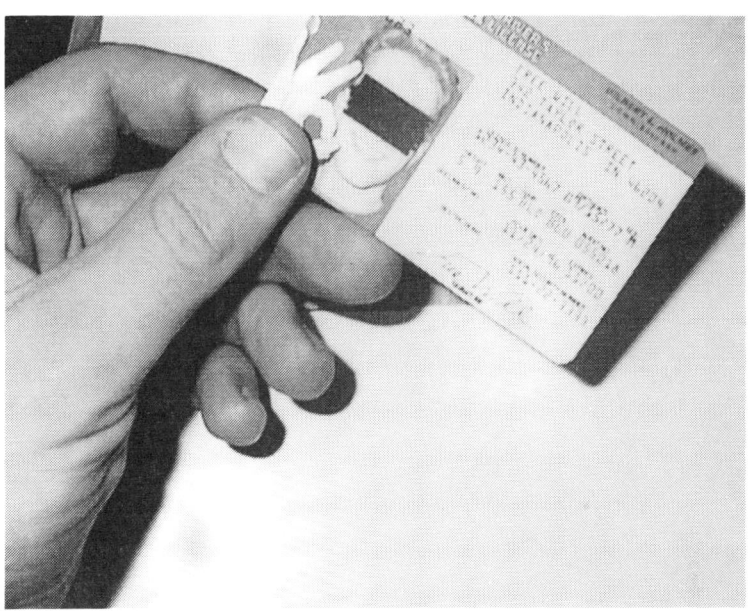

**HAVING TROUBLE MAKING THE CORNERS
LOOK GOOD?**

A corner-rounder can be purchased at the local camera shop.
For about $40, it ensures that the corners are perfect every time.

How to Make Driver's Licenses and Other ID on Your Home Computer

Step 7
   Paste the front of the license to the Teslin card using Elmer's Mucilage glue. Wait two minutes for the glue to set.

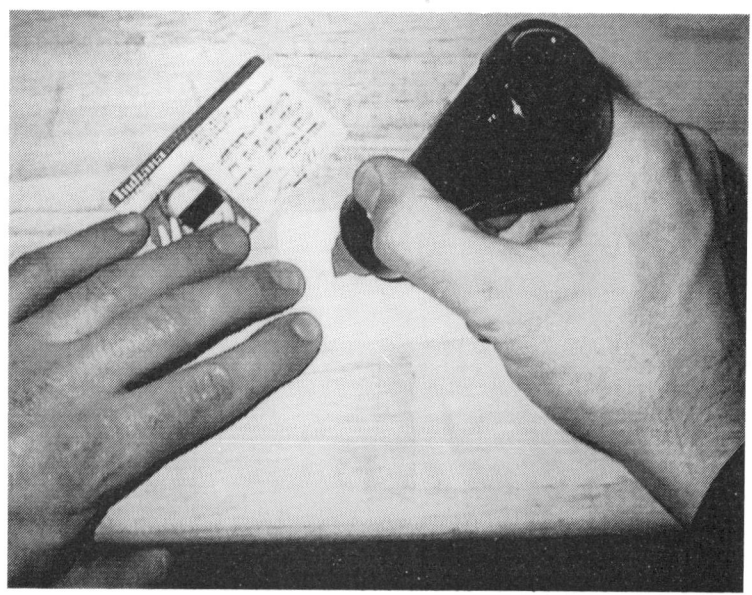

Step 8
   Use the ruler and the Exacto knife to cut the Teslin card to size. A credit card or phone card with rounded corners can be used as an aid for cutting the rounded corners.

*Chapter Eleven
Printing, Cutting, and Laminating
Structure One Licenses*

Step 9

Paste the back of the license to the Teslin card using Elmer's Mucilage glue. Wait two minutes for the glue to set.

Step 10

Slip the lamination pouch over the license — make sure that the license is centered. Insert the license into the lamination sleeve. After the laminator heats up, run the lamination sleeve or card through the laminator three times. Remove the card and set it aside for a minute or two.

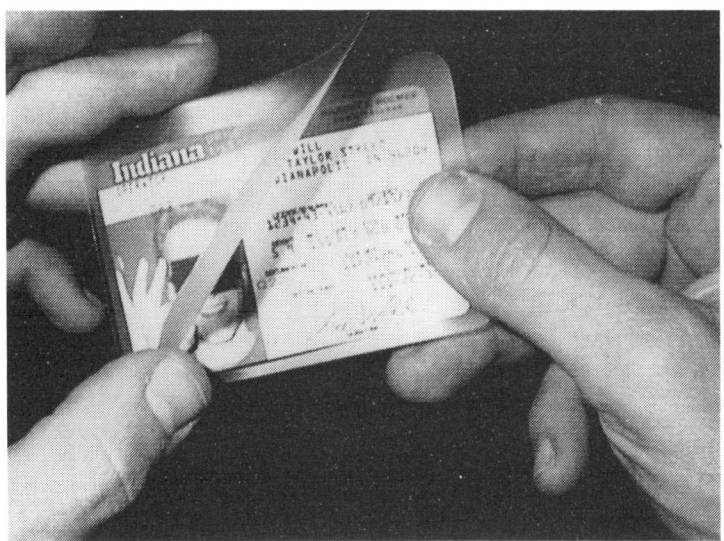

How to Make Driver's Licenses and Other ID on Your Home Computer

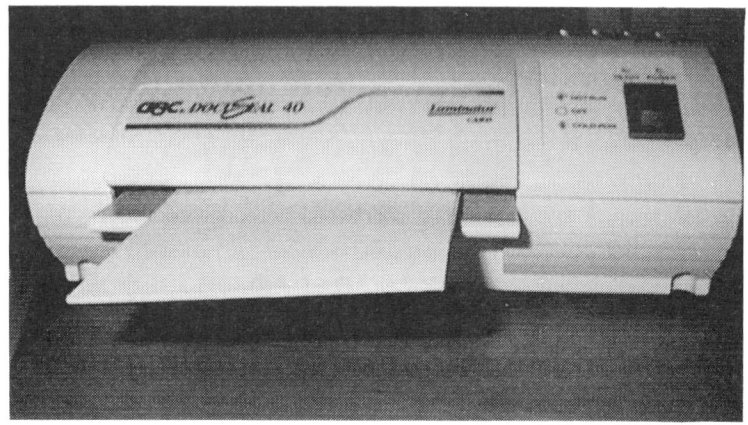

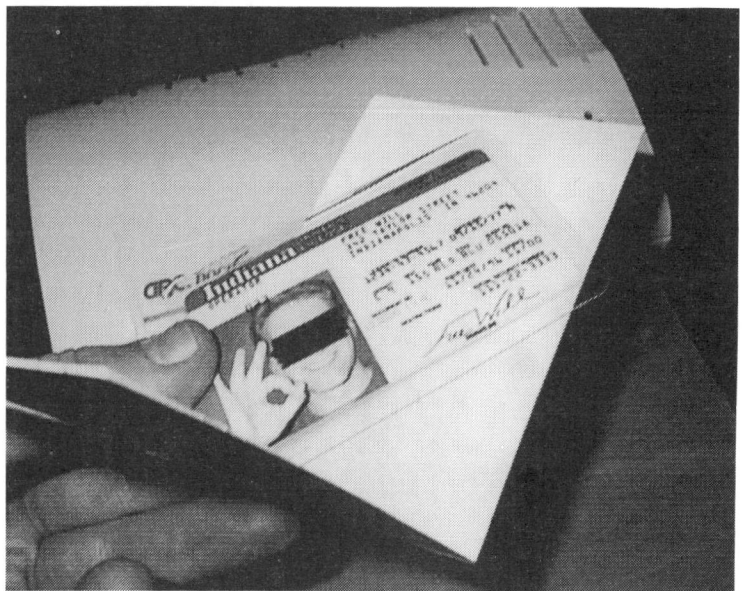

Step 11
Now it's time to assess the lamination. The following is a list of potential problems and the ways to correct them:

A. The License Is Not Centered in the Lamination Pouch. There's no way to fix this problem without compromising the license. Return to Step 1. (Next time make sure the information card is centered before running it through the laminator.)

B. The License Lamination Pouch Is Bubbly. Try running the license through the laminator a few more times. If this doesn't work, then there's no way to fix this problem without compromising the license. Return to Step 1.

C. The Edge of the Lamination Pouch Is Separated. The laminator may not have been hot enough during the original lamination. Reconfirm that the laminator is at the proper temperature, then run the license through the laminator a few more times. If this doesn't fix the problem, return to Step 1.

Step 12
Allow the license to cool off for five minutes. Sand the edge of the lamination with 600-grit sandpaper until the edges are completely smooth.

Step 13
Lightly sand the front and back of the license with 600-grit sandpaper to give it that "lived-in" look. Don't sand it too much — just rub it enough to take the shine off.

Chapter Twelve
Printing, Cutting, and Laminating Structure Two Licenses

This chapter provides step-by-step instructions for completing the Structure Two license.

Required Materials

The following materials are required for the completion of this chapter:

- a 10-millimeter lamination pouch (with or without a magnetic strip)
- a Teslin card
- card laminator
- photo-quality paper
- Elmer's Mucilage glue
- an Exacto knife, cutting board, and metal-edged ruler
- 600-grit sandpaper
- any credit card or phone card with rounded edges

How to Make Driver's Licenses and Other ID on Your Home Computer

76

Step 1
Load the front and back of the license template into Photoshop.

Step 2
Select *Image* from the menu bar. Select *Image Size* from the pull-down menu. Confirm that the *Resolution* is set to 1200 (pixels/inch).

Step 3
Press the *SHIFT* and *CONTROL* and *P* keys simultaneously. Select *Properties*. Configure the printer to print on photo-quality glossy paper at the maximum

Chapter Twelve
Printing, Cutting, and Laminating
Structure Two Licenses

resolution (this will vary based on the printer so it will not be covered here — consult the printer's owner's manual).

Step 4

Load the printer with photo-quality paper. Press the *CONTROL* and *P* keys simultaneously. Click on the *OK* button. This will print the license.

Step 5

Although the license printout should be perfect at this point, quickly check the quality as discussed in Chapter Four, Step 1l.

How to Make Driver's Licenses and Other ID on Your Home Computer

Step 6

Lay the license printout on the cutting board. Use the ruler and the Exacto knife to cut the front of the license out. Remember that in Structure Two licenses, the front information card is centered on the Teslin card. The rounded corners of a credit card or phone card can be used as an aid for cutting the rounded corners.

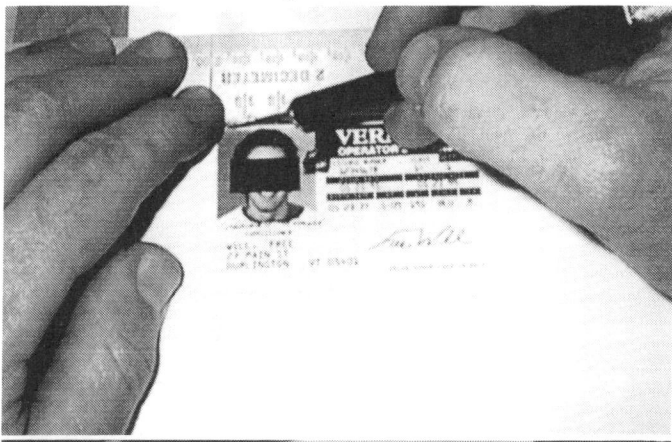

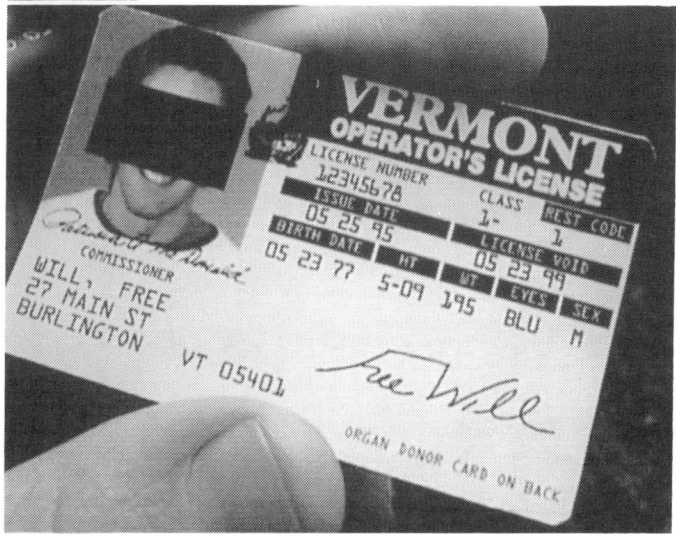

Chapter Twelve
Printing, Cutting, and Laminating
Structure Two Licenses

HAVING TROUBLE MAKING THE CORNERS LOOK GOOD?

A corner-rounder can be purchased at the local camera shop. For about $40, it ensures that the corners are perfect every time.

Step 7

Lay the license printout on the cutting board. Use the ruler and the Exacto knife to cut the back of the license out. Remember that in Structure Two licenses, the back information card covers the entire Teslin card. The rounded corners of a credit card or phone card can be used as an aid for cutting the rounded corners.

Step 8

Paste the front of the license to the Teslin card using Elmer's Mucilage glue. Wait two minutes for the glue to set.

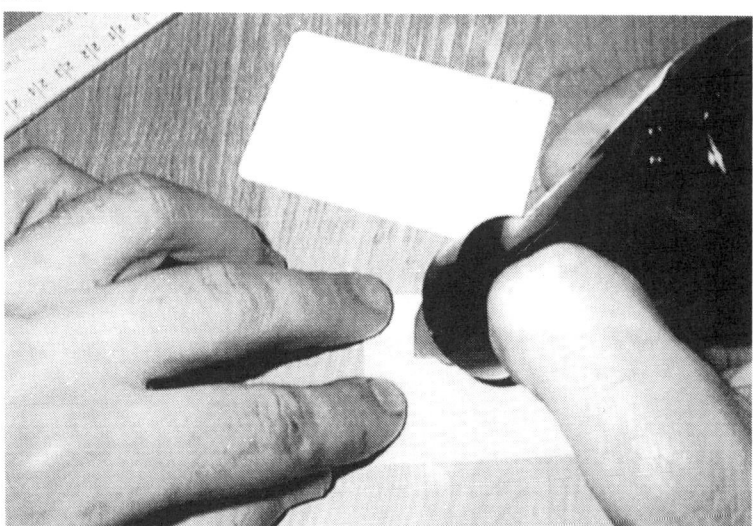

How to Make Driver's Licenses and Other ID on Your Home Computer

Step 9
Paste the back of the license to the Teslin card using Elmer's Mucilage glue. Wait two minutes for the glue to set.

Step 10
Slip the lamination pouch over the license — make sure that the license is centered. Insert the license into the lamination sleeve. Run the lamination sleeve or card through the laminator three times. Remove the card and set it aside for a minute or two.

Chapter Twelve
Printing, Cutting, and Laminating
Structure Two Licenses
81

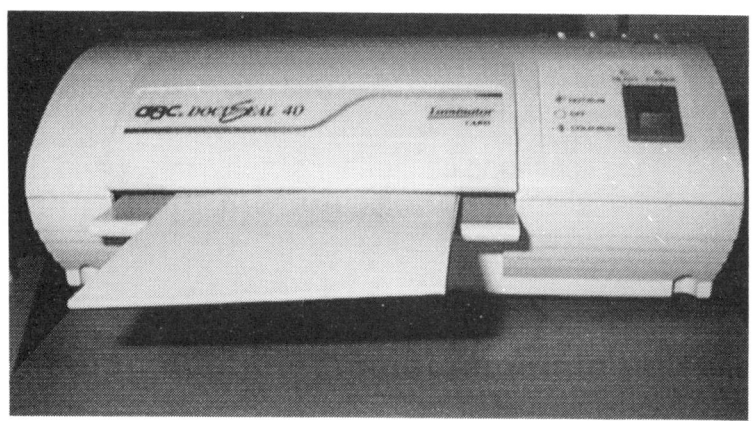

Step 11
Now it's time to assess the lamination. The following is a list of potential problems and the ways to correct them:

A. The License Is Not Centered in the Lamination Pouch. There's no way to fix this problem without compromising the license. Return to Step 1. (Next time make sure the information card is centered before running it through the laminator.)

B. The License Lamination Pouch Is Bubbly. Try running the license through the laminator a few more times. If this doesn't work, then there's no way to fix this problem without compromising the license. Return to Step 1.

C. The Edge of the Lamination Pouch Is Separated. The laminator may not have been hot enough during the original lamination. Reconfirm that the laminator is at the proper temperature, then run the license through the laminator a few more times. If this doesn't fix the problem, return to Step 1.

Step 12
Allow the license to cool off for ten minutes. Sand the edge of the lamination with 600-grit sandpaper until the edges are completely smooth.

Step 13
Lightly sand the front and back of the license to give it that "lived-in" look. Don't sand it too much — just rub it enough to take the shine off.

Chapter Thirteen
Printing, Cutting, and Laminating Structure Three Licenses

This chapter provides step-by-step instructions for completing the Structure Three license.

Required Materials

The following materials are required for the completion of this chapter:

- a 5-millimeter lamination pouch (with or without a magnetic strip)
- two Teslin cards
- card laminator
- Elmer's Mucilage glue
- an Exacto knife, cutting board, and metal-edged ruler
- 600-grit sandpaper
- any credit card or phone card with rounded edges

Step 1
Load the front of the license template into Photoshop.

How to Make Driver's Licenses and Other ID on Your Home Computer

84

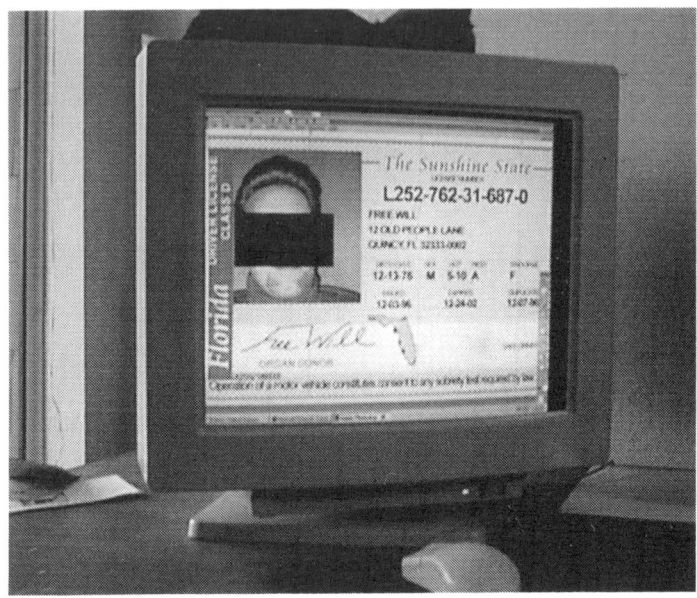

Step 2
Select *Image* from the menu bar. Select *Image Size* from the pull-down menu. Confirm that the *Resolution* is set to 1200 (pixels/inch).

Step 3
Press the *SHIFT* and *CONTROL* and *P* keys simultaneously. Select *Properties*. Configure the printer to print on photo-quality glossy film at the maximum resolution. (This will vary based on the printer so it will not be covered here — consult the printer's owner's manual.)

Step 4
Load the printer with Teslin. Press the *CONTROL* and *P* keys simultaneously. Click on the *OK* button. This will print the front of the license.

Chapter Thirteen
Printing, Cutting and Laminating
Structure Three Licenses
85

Note: Lining up the Teslin can be difficult. A little bit of patience helps here.

IS THE PRINTOUT ALIGNED CORRECTLY?

Examine the card. If the image is not perfectly aligned on the Teslin card, discard the Teslin and return to Step 4.

Step 5
Wait two minutes for the ink to dry. Carefully remove the Teslin card from the paper. Make sure not to touch the ink — it may smear. Set the card aside.

Step 6
Load the back of the license template into Photoshop.

How to Make Driver's Licenses and Other ID on Your Home Computer

Step 7
Load the printer with Teslin. Press the *CONTROL* and *P* keys simultaneously. Click on the *OK* button. This will print the back of the license.

IS THE PRINTOUT ALIGNED CORRECTLY?

Examine the card. If the image is not perfectly aligned on the Teslin card, discard the Teslin and return to Step 7.

Step 8
Wait two minutes for the ink to dry. Carefully remove the Teslin card from the paper. Make sure not to touch the ink — it may smear.

Step 9
Glue the two Teslin cards together using Elmer's Mucilage glue. Make sure that the front and the back have the same orientation. Also minimize touching the cards — the ink may smear.

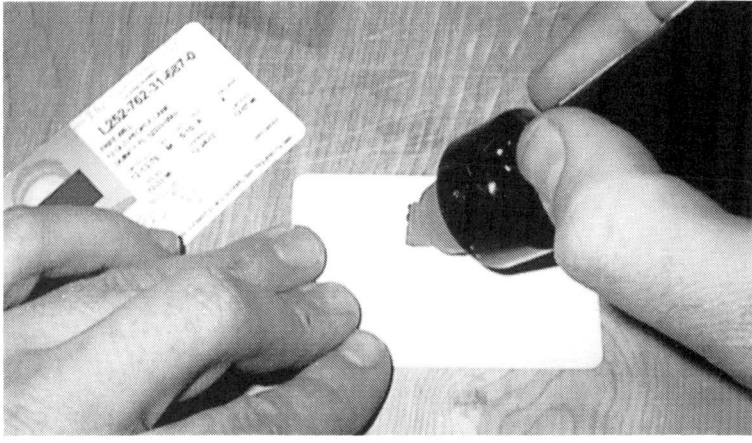

Chapter Thirteen
Printing, Cutting and Laminating
Structure Three Licenses

Step 10

Slip the lamination pouch over the license, making sure that the license is centered. Insert the license into the lamination sleeve. Run the lamination sleeve and card through the laminator three times. Remove the card and set it aside for a minute or two.

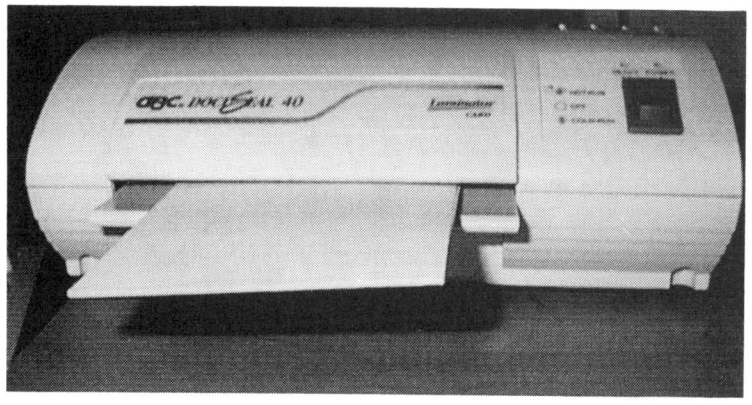

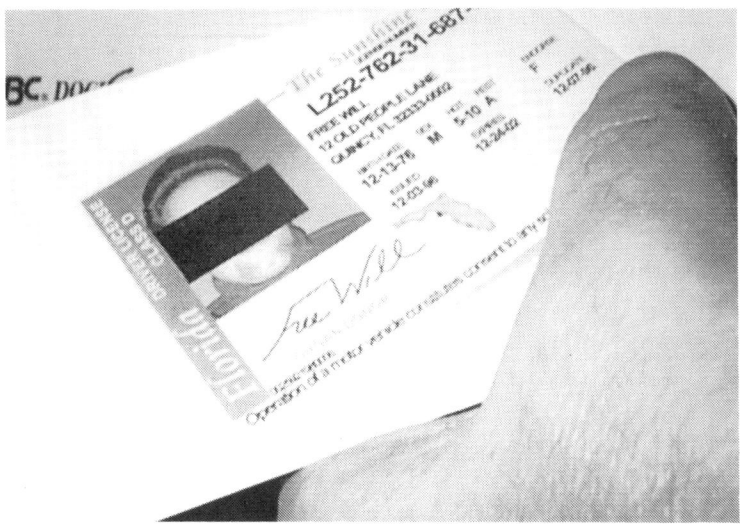

How to Make Driver's Licenses and Other ID on Your Home Computer

Step 11

Now it's time to assess the lamination. The following is a list of potential problems and the ways to correct them:

A. The License Is Not Centered in the Lamination Pouch. There's no way to fix this problem without compromising the license. Return to Step 1. Next time make sure the information card is centered before running it through the laminator.

B. The License Lamination Pouch Is Bubbly. Try running the license through the laminator a few more times. If this doesn't work, then there's no way to fix this problem without compromising the license. Return to Step 1.

C. The Edge of the Lamination Pouch Is Separated. The laminator may not have been hot enough during the original lamination. Reconfirm that the laminator is at the proper temperature, then run the license through the laminator a few more times. If this doesn't fix the problem, return to Step 1.

D. The Lamination Pouch Is Visible Beyond the Edge of the Teslin. Use the Exacto knife and ruler to trim any excess lamination. Structure Three licenses should have no lamination overlapping the Teslin edges.

*Chapter Thirteen
Printing, Cutting and Laminating
Structure Three Licenses*

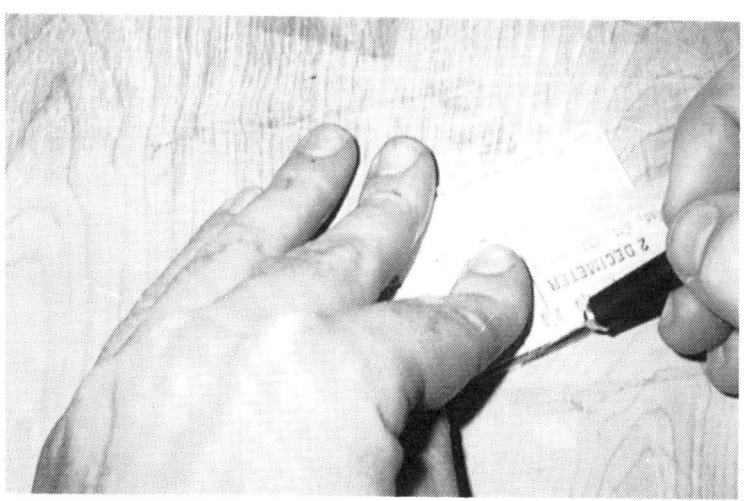

Step 12
Allow the license to cool off for ten minutes. Sand the edge of the lamination with 600-grit sandpaper until the edges are completely smooth.

Step 13
Lightly sand the front and back of the license to give it that "lived-in" look. Don't sand it too much, just rub it a few times to take the shine off.

Chapter Fourteen
Back-up ID

When using out-of-state ID, a back-up ID is essential. If the person assessing the ID is unsure of its validity, he will ask for a back-up. Back-up IDs can be easily manufactured using the techniques discussed in this book. The back-up ID required depends highly on the user's age and expected ID use.

> **HOW ABOUT A LIBRARY CARD AS A BACK-UP ID?**
>
> If you're thinking of acquiring a library card, don't. It is common knowledge that anyone can get a library card in any name. Flashing a library card at someone when they ask for a back-up ID is more likely to hurt your credibility than help it.

Under 21

For people who are under 21 and just trying to get into a bar, a college ID will do the trick. There are many college-ID templates available on the Web or you can just completely make it up. College IDs are almost always of exceedingly poor quality and are very easy to make.

Privacy Seekers

For people interested in protecting personal privacy, an employee ID is an excellent choice.

The employee ID should contain the following details:

- Company logo: Go to any company's Web site and download a few of their symbols. Don't make it anything too well known or it might raise questions.
- Your picture: Don't use the same picture that's on the license. Consider using a different color background for variety. If possible wear dress clothes.
- Name.
- Employee number: Just make up at least six alpha-numeric characters.
- Lamination with a magnetic stripe pouch.

Chapter Fourteen
Back-up ID

Puchase an alligator clip and ID holder to house the ID.

One More Can't Hurt

A third ID will provide additional comfort. A Blockbuster Video card is easily reproducible and easily recognizable by the person assessing the ID. If the person checking is still on the edge after seeing the first two IDs, the familiar Blockbuster card will almost always sway him.

Chapter Fifteen
Evaluating the Completed License: Is It Good Enough?

This chapter discusses evaluation of the completed license.*

Step 1
Use the Test Form on the following two pages to confirm that the ID is perfect before you take the ID "public."

*__Note:__ Tests and assessments performed in Chapters One through Fourteen will not be repeated here.

Test Form

Procedure	Expected Result	Pass/ Fail?	What to do if It fails
Closely examine the edges of the ID. Make sure there are no gaps between the laminated layers.	There are no gaps between the laminated layers.		Run the ID through the laminator a few more times. Reassess.
Rub a finger along all four edges and corners, make sure they are smooth.	All four edges and corners are smooth.		Sand the edges and corners smooth with 600-grit sandpaper.
Hold the ID at the left and right edges. Bend the ID so that the center deflects about an inch, first in one direction then in the other. Verify that the ID: • "bounces back" to its original position • doesn't make a crackling noise • doesn't delaminate	The ID bounces back to its original position. The ID doesn't make a crackling noise. The ID doesn't delaminate.		Discard the ID and return to Chapter Nine.

Chapter Fifteen
Evaluating the Completed License: Is It Good Enough?

Test Form
(Continued)

Procedure	Expected Result	Pass/ Fail?	What to do if It fails
Twist the ID. Verify that the ID: • "bounces back" to its original position • doesn't make a crackling noise • doesn't delaminate	The ID bounces back to its original position. The ID doesn't make a crackling noise. The ID doesn't delaminate.		Discard the ID and return to Chapter Nine.
Examine the lamination covering the front and back of the ID. Verify that the laminate is not burned, melted, discolored, or bubbly.	The laminate is not burned, melted, discolored, or bubbly.		Discard the ID and return to Chapter Nine.

Step 2

Find a liquor store near a college where everyone gets carded. Look for a store with a "wall of shame" (a place where confiscated fake IDs are posted, usually behind the counter). If there is a "wall of shame," clerks take pride in confiscating questionable IDs and are very good at detecting them.

Buy a case or two of the cheapest beer in the store; this is a typical underage move. When the clerk asks for ID, present the fake ID. If he accepts the fake ID, anyone

How to Make Driver's Licenses and Other ID on Your Home Computer

will. Usually if he identifies it as fake, he'll just take it away. Don't shop at a liquor store if there is a police officer posted at the door.

Chapter Sixteen
Using the License Intelligently

1. *Never* mix legitimate and fake IDs in the same wallet.
2. *Never* present the ID to a state or government official.
3. *Never* present the ID to anyone if a state or government official is nearby.
4. *Never* sell fake IDs or manufacture them for friends.
5. *Never* get confrontational with someone if they refuse the ID. Simply thank them, take the ID (if possible) and walk away.
6. *Never* carry the fake ID unless you're going to use it.
7. *Always* know everything about the identity you've created. Besides memorizing all of the information on the ID, make sure you know:
   - a little about the state/town on the ID — especially if you're from a well-known city, such as San Francisco, California, or an exotic place, like Alaska
   - your astrological sign — it's a common bouncer question

How to Make Driver's Licenses and Other ID on Your Home Computer

- why you're in town — people may ask when they see your out-of-state license

8. *Always* hide the fake ID when not in use.

Appendix A

Appendix A

Photoshop Tool Menu

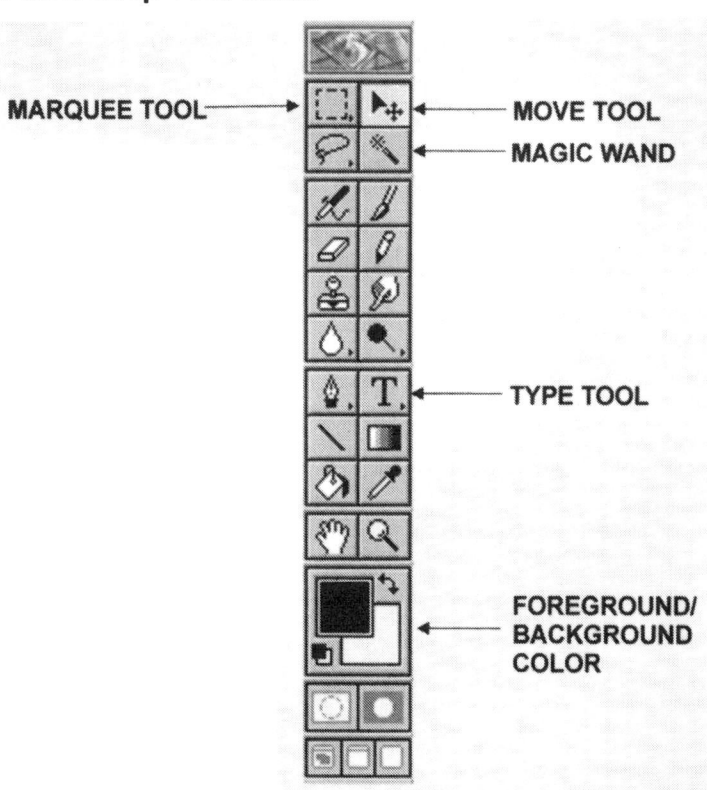

How to Make Driver's Licenses and Other ID
on Your Home Computer

102

Photoshop Color Balance Menu

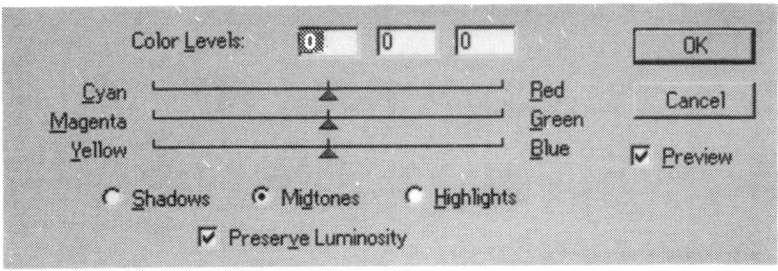

Brightness/Contrast Window

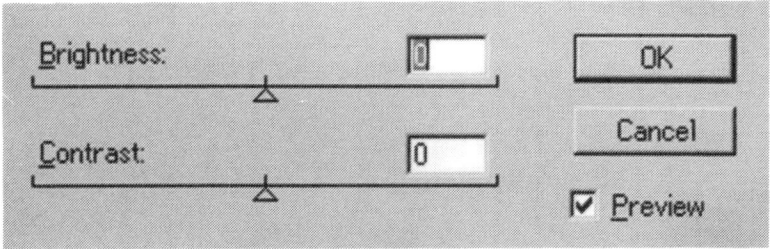

Appendix A

103

Photoshop Image Size Window

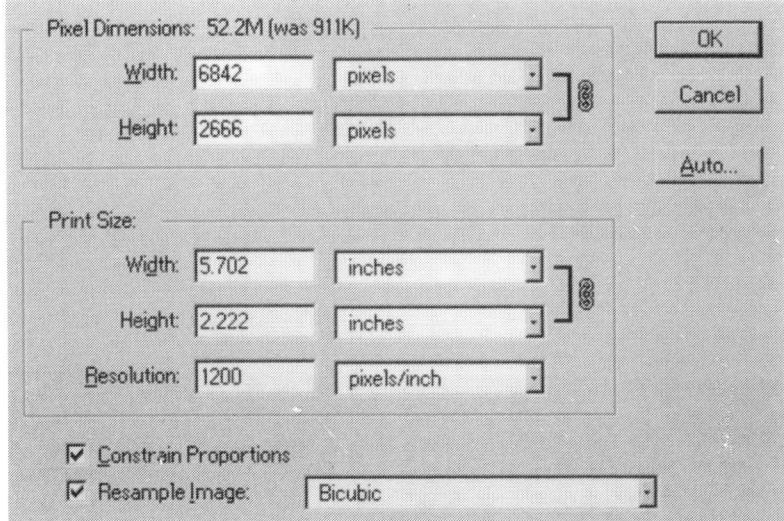

Photoshop Type Tool Window

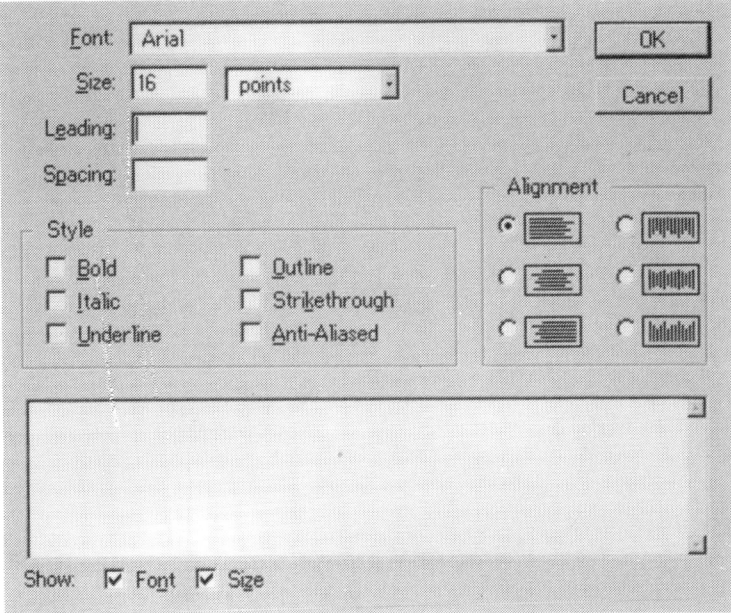

Photoshop Rotate Canvas Window

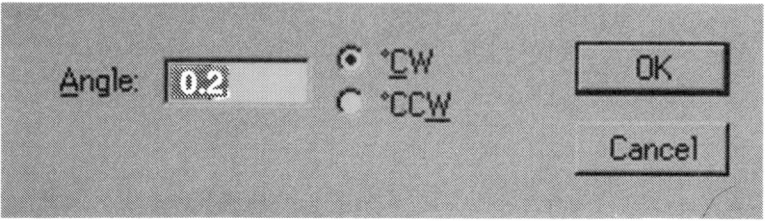

YOU WILL ALSO WANT TO READ:

- 61152 **DOCUMENT FRAUD AND OTHER CRIMES OF DECEPTION,** *by Jesse M. Greenwald.* Written by a 20-year practitioner of document fraud with 22 felonies and five prison terms to his credit, this book clearly explains: computer equipment the forger needs, and alternative methods of acquiring it; necessary software; the notary stamp; how the forger fabricates checks, stock certificates, trust and quitclaim deeds, vehicle titles, and bonded credit cards; methods the forger employs to obtain alternative identification; and much more. *1997, 5½ x 8½, 152 pp, illustrated, soft cover.* $15.00.

- 61163 **IDENTITY THEFT: The Cybercrime of the Millennium,** *by John Q. Newman.* Your most valuable possession is not your house, your car, or your collection of antique jewelry. Your most valuable possession is what makes you *you* — your identity. Each year, more than 500,000 Americans fall victim to identity theft, and that number is rising. A stolen identity can mean the loss of your job, your credit rating, your friends, and in extreme cases, can result in a prison sentence for a crime you did not commit. This book is the most effective tool in your arsenal against the cyberspace thief. Use it to protect your identity — while you still have one. *1999, 5½ x 8½, 106 pp, soft cover.* $12.00.

- 61168 **THE ID FORGER: Birth Certificates & Other Documents Explained,** *by John Q. Newman. The ID Forger* covers in step-by-step detail all of the classic and modern high-tech methods of forging the commonly used identification documents. Chapters include: The use of homemade documents; Old-fashioned forgery; Computer forgery; Birth certificate basics; and Other miscellaneous document forgery. *1999, 5½ x 8½, 110 pp, soft cover.* $15.00.

Loompanics Unlimited
PO Box 1197
Port Townsend, WA 98368

DLID1

Please send me the books I have checked above. I have enclosed $_____ which includes $5.95 for shipping and handling of the first $25.00 ordered. Add an additional $1 shipping for each additional $25 ordered. Washington residents include 8.2% sales tax.

Name _____

Address _____

City/State/Zip _____

VISA, Discover, and MasterCard accepted.
1-800-380-2230 for credit card orders *only.*
24 hours a day, 7 days a week.
Web site: www.loompanics.com

"Thank you very much for such prompt service. Keep it up with your wonderful titles, too. I believe this is the start of a wonderful business relationship." — J. Watt

"You guys are nuts... but I love it. My only problem is trying to figure out which books to order! Your catalog shouts freedom. Keep it up." — Biff

"Best catalog on the planet." — S. Scully

"Keep up the good work. I don't buy as much as I'd like to from you (just don't have time to read everything I'd like) but I enjoy the catalogs and the knowledge that you are there. Thanks." — Dave

"I've ordered from you for over ten years now. I did a search and found your web site on the Internet, so I thought I'd order some books. Let me say you've always been a great company to deal with and I am very satisfied with your company. Furthermore, you site is QUICK and EASY to access. Thanks!" — RMR

"Thanks for the info. When Lynnette introduced me to the catalogue, I thought that she was just freaky, but as I had a chance to peruse the info, I found myself falling in love with the catalogue. Thanks so much!" — Higgi, the Great and Wonderful

"Thanks for the great books and service in the last twenty years!" — WC

THE BEST BOOK CATALOG IN THE WORLD!!!

We offer hard-to-find books on the world's most unusual subjects. Here are a few of the topics covered IN DEPTH in our exciting new catalog:

- *Hiding/Concealment of physical objects! A complete section of the best books ever written on hiding things.*
- *Fake ID/Alternate Identities! The most comprehensive selection of books on this little-known subject ever offered for sale! You have to see it to believe it!*
- *Investigative/Undercover methods and techniques! Professional secrets known only to a few, now revealed to you to use! Actual police manuals on shadowing and surveillance!*
- *And much, much more, including Locks and Lock Picking, Self-Defense, Intelligence Increase, Life Extension, Money-Making Opportunities, Human Oddities, Exotic Weapons, Sex, Drugs, Anarchism, and more!*

Our book catalog is over 200 pages, 8½ x 11, packed with more than 800 of the most controversial and unusual books ever printed! You can order every book listed! Periodic supplements keep you posted on the LATEST titles available!!! Our catalog is **$5.00,** including shipping and handling.

Our book catalog is truly THE BEST BOOK CATALOG IN THE WORLD! Order yours today. You will be very pleased, we know.

**LOOMPANICS UNLIMITED
PO BOX 1197
PORT TOWNSEND, WA 98368**

Name _____

Address _____

City/State/Zip _____

We accept Visa, Discover, and MasterCard. For credit card orders *only,* call 1-800-380-2230, 24 hours a day, 7 days a week.

Web site: www.loompanics.com